7 DAY
BUSINESS PLAN

CARL J. GRAY III

CONTENTS

ACKNOWLEDGMENTS

I really didn't want to do an "Acknowledgments" page because I would inevitably leave someone out. But how bad would it be to leave EVERYONE out? EXACTLY. So many people have influenced, helped, and poured into me to help me get to this point that well, I'm just going to make a list! IF I missed you, charge it to my head not my heart. Here we go:

The Most High **YHWH**

Desiree Lynn, Prophet Mom, Ma, Dad, Kevin, Keith, Markesia, Joshua & Sherah Power, The Ramseurs, Bro. CJ, Mr. Murray, Mr. Bazilio, Dea. Caleb, Leonard & Winona Barnes, Mr. Jon Mangana, Aunt D, Aunt Barbara, Aunt Venetta, Uncle Craig, Mr. Shabazz, Student Leaders, IYKYK, New Face, All City, Dr. Wendell Hall, Mark Brown, Dr. Raphael Denbow. **See, what I mean?!?!?**

In Memoriam: Grandma (Mamie), Grandma Freda, Grandad, Mamadear & Papa Thompson, Larry "Chief" Cherry, Mrs. Murray, Kenneth L. Riddle, Marvin Jones, James "Trackey" Simon, Jeff, Donnie "CYCO" Barnes, Pashence , Briyah

This book isn't just for reading!

I don't expect anyone to just sit down and read through it without taking action. This includes doing the workbook that comes with each chapter. (you can download the workbook at www.7daybusinessplan.com/workbook)

If you have any questions or need any help with understanding the material, I'm here to help. You can email me at cgray@prototypeconsultinggroup.com and I'll get back to you as soon as possible.

Also, if you'd like a more personal touch, feel free to book a free consultation at https://discovery.launchwithcarl.com. During this time we can discuss your business plan in more detail and if needed make adjustments where necessary.

Let's make sure your 7-day journey is successful! Don't hesitate to contact me for assistance anytime during your journey so that together we can achieve success!

P.S. Don't get frustrated if it takes you more than 7 days. Go at your own pace and reach out if you need help

To reach me directly, email **cgray@PrototypeConsultingGroup.com**

"Proper planning and preparation prevent poor performance."
Stephen Keague

INTRODUCTION

So, here's the rundown. EACH successful company has a plan. Whether it's formalized (having been written and authorized), informal (based on regular practices with no full codification) or just in the head of the owner, every business has a strategy and direction. The stronger the plan, the more important it is that it is recorded

The effectiveness of any strategy depends entirely on how well it can be distributed and put into action. The more significant and complex an organization is, the more crucial it is that a plan be written, formalized, and implemented.

The primary benefit of having a written plan is that it forces the business owner to think through all aspects of the business and what is necessary for success. It also allows input from others, which can be invaluable.

Once the basic structure and operation of the business are down on paper (or in pixels), it becomes much easier to make changes and adapt as the business grows. A plan also serves as a road map to success, providing benchmarks and milestones that can be used to measure progress.

The process of creating a business plan can be just as important as the finished product. Brainstorming with employees, partners, and other stakeholders gets everyone on the same page and ensures that the final product reflects the needs and goals of the business.

The 7 Day Business Plan is designed to get you thinking about all aspects of your business, from the big-picture items like vision and mission to the minutiae of daily operations. It's not only a valuable exercise for new business owners; it can also be helpful for seasoned entrepreneurs who are looking to take their business in a new direction.

The first step is to set aside some time each day for the next week to work on your business plan. You don't have to complete it all at once; in fact, it's probably better if you don't. Dedicate an hour or two each day to thinking about one specific aspect of your business. On day one, for example, you might focus on your company's history and what led you to start the business. Day two could be devoted to your target market, and so on.

WHY DO YOU NEED A BUSINESS PLAN?

"The first casualty of war is the plan" - Unknown
"Planning is everything. The plan is nothing"
– Dwight Eisenhower, Former US President

With quotes like these, one could think *"what's the use of even creating a business plan?" Well, I'll tell you.*

If you are starting a business, or if you have an existing business, a business plan is essential. It can help you set goals, track your progress, and attract investors.

A business plan is a document that outlines your business goals and how you plan to achieve them. It can be used to attract investors, secure loans, and track your company's progress. A well-crafted business plan is an invaluable tool for any business.

Experts agree that a business plan is critical for any business. It can help you attract investors, secure loans, and track your company's progress.

Other benefits of a well-crafted business plan include:

- To establish the fundamental viability of a project.

- To define your products, services and customers and assess competitors.

- To map out the business model, the goals and the strategy used to achieve them.

- To evaluate initial startup costs

- To communicate to others (banks, investors, partners, etc.) the business idea.

A business plan will help you build a business that will support you financially, have an impact on those around you, and leave a lasting legacy you can be proud of.

But can't you just get things up and running and make adjustments on the fly? Can't you sort of learn as you go? Yes, you can do those things, but the odds that your business will fail are much higher.

See, a business plan functions as a "crystal ball" of sorts. It helps you to peer into the future and predict different outcomes. Though it's certainly not perfect, it helps you map out where you currently are and where you're headed.

Specifically, a business plan helps you to:

- **Estimate total startup costs** -Once you know the approximate costs, you can determine whether you'll need to raise funds from investors.

- **Project revenues and profits-** By forcing you to define both your market and how much of that market you expect to reach, a business plan helps you estimate potential revenues and profits.

- **Convince investors-** A business plan shows investors that you have a clear and defined strategy for achieving success. If this strategy isn't present, investors won't want to finance your business.

- **Compete from the start-** As part of your business plan, you'll identify key gaps in the marketplace which your company will fill. This allows you to hit the ground running.

- **Anticipate challenges-** When you create your business plan, you'll look ahead and try to identify any potential problems you might encounter. This prepares you to address these issues if they do arise.

Are you starting to see the value of a business plan?

It may be helpful to think of it in construction terms. If you were building a new house, you would use a plan, right? If you didn't use a plan, you'd encounter all sorts of issues. Wires and pipes and even walls could end up in the wrong places. A building plan keeps you on track.

In the same way, **a business plan helps keep you on track.** It ensures that you focus your attention on the right things and helps you avoid mistakes that could sink you.

Writing for The Balance, Alyssa Gregory notes:

...one study found that entrepreneurs who write formal plans are 16% more likely to achieve viability than the otherwise identical non-planning entrepreneurs. Other studies have shown that while completing a business plan is not a guarantee of success, it does indicate that the type of entrepreneur who completes a business plan is also more likely to run a successful business.

So how do you write a business plan? What things need to be included?

That's what this guide is all about. We're going to walk you step-by-step through the process of creating a solid business plan. By the end, you'll know exactly what to do to create your own plan.

Ready?

Let's dive in.

BEFORE YOU START

I get it, you're an entrepreneur! Just like me, you've been waiting for this moment for what seems like forever. You're chomping at the bit to start creating your business plan, and that's a good thing. But before you get started there are a few things to consider.

Unfortunately, many business plans are wildly unrealistic. It's not hard to understand why. It's exciting to start a new business. You've got big dreams, big goals, and huge amounts of ambition. You want to make a serious impact.

The problem is that this excitement often causes entrepreneurs to massively overestimate how successful they'll be and underestimate the problems they'll encounter.

In other cases, some underestimate how successful they can be and fail to plan what will happen when they easily overcome obstacles and have their growth stunted.

The primary key is **to be realistic.** Remember, ultimately, you're the one who's going to be pouring time and money into your venture. Before you launch, you want to be relatively confident that you have a good chance of succeeding.

Jeff Haden says:

> *For many entrepreneurs, developing a business plan is the first step in the process of deciding whether to actually start a business. Determining if an idea fails on paper can help a prospective founder avoid wasting time and money on a business with no realistic hope of success.*

So, in many ways, a business plan should help you decide whether your idea will pan out. This doesn't mean that you need to anticipate every risk. There's no way you can do that. However, **it's important to be thoughtful, methodical, and careful as you put together your plan.**

It's possible that you may put together your business plan and then realize that the potential outcome isn't as bright as you initially thought. You might realize that the competition is much tougher than you realized or that the market is smaller than you anticipated. In which case, you make adjustments, regroup, or even get help.

That's okay. In fact, it's a good thing. It forces you to go back to the drawing board and reevaluate. It's better to realize these things before you launch your business and spend tens of thousands of dollars. Sometimes we get so connected to the 'pride of ownership' that comes with birthing and idea, that we need help seeing where it can be improved. That's where a consultant can help. We'll talk about that later though.

At a minimum, your business plan should convince you that you'll succeed. When you logically evaluate all the data you've assembled in your plan, you should feel confident that you're going to achieve your goals. When you're confident, you're more likely to convince potential investors to back you too.

So, with all that said, be patient as you assemble your plan. Take the necessary time to do the market research, analyze your financial needs, and map out your strategy for the future.

Is it a pain? It all depends on how you look at it. If you see it as the thing that's preventing you from getting started, then creating a business plan will seem like a necessary evil. But **if you view it as building a foundation for a successful, lasting business, it changes your perspective.**

Shameless Plug: One of my products "4 Days to launch" guides new entrepreneurs through a four-day process where they launch the product and make a profit all while gathering critical data for their business plan. This not only helps to validate the information you THINK will be correct. But you ALSO are making money. Which helps give a better perspective to the planning process.

As you see, a business plan is vitally important to your success.

Next, let's look at what all you'll want to put into your business plan.

As a special gift to you, I've created a companion workbook that contains all the steps, forms, and checklists you need to get your business up and running in seven days. It also includes additional resources for any new business owner – from startup costs to financial management and other considerations – so that you can launch your business with confidence.

This workbook will help make sure that you have everything covered when starting your business, so that you can become a successful business owner in just seven days. With my advice and the tools provided in this book and its companion workbook, anyone can take that first step toward becoming an entrepreneur.

Visit https://7daybusinessplan.com/workbook to claim your free companion book!

"Often our businesses are in our mind. a bunch of ideas that we just know are great and we're very passionate about. it's very important that we bring all of those ideas together to form a foundation to build upon. this will help us to stay focused throughout the entire process."

DAY ONE - FOUNDATION

1.1 NAME YOUR BUSINESS

Chances are, you've had the name of your business on your mind for years. This normally immediately follows the idea. If you don't have a name, here are some things to consider in developing a name.

1. Make sure it communicates what your business does for the customer.
2. Choose a name that appeals not only to you and your emotions and desires but primarily to the kind of customers you are trying to attract. *Remember, it's about your customer, not about your ego.*
3. Choose a comforting or familiar name that conjures up pleasant memories so customers respond to your business on an emotional level.
4. Avoid names that are long or so laced with innuendo that it takes a genius to understand.
5. Stay away from cute puns that only you understand; inside jokes don't attract the outside public.

6. Don't use the word "Inc." or any other abbreviation that doesn't actually pally to your business (e.g. don't use "Inc" after your name unless your company is actually incorporated.)
7. Choose a name that can easily be translated into a domain name for your website.
8. Make sure you have the legal rights to use the name before investing too much money in marketing it. Conduct a search of state and federal databases to make sure the name isn't trademarked or copyrighted by another business.
9. Get feedback from friends, family, and potential customers before making your final decision. Ask them what the name makes them think of and if it would make them want to do business with you.
10. Have fun with it! Choosing a name for your business should be an enjoyable experience. After all, this is the beginning of your entrepreneurial journey!

While it is very possible that you can have a name that doesn't follow any of these conventions and have success, (see Google, Kinkos, Apple) it's a lot easier to resonate with potential customers, especially in this day and age, if you have a name that, at the very least, subconsciously triggers something in the mind.

 The bottom line is this: the name of your business should be something that you're proud of, but it also needs to be practical and make sense for both you and your customers. With a little bit of thought and creativity, you can find the perfect name for your business!

If you haven't already, you can download the companion workbook that contains a worksheet on how to choose the perfect name for your business, visit https://www.7businessdayplan.com/workbook NOW to get it

1.2   MISSION STATEMENT

Your mission statement should speak to the core of your business. What you believe in, the quality of service that you will bring, how people will feel when after they do business with you. It should be very specific when speaking of goals, but not focus a whole lot on methodologies. A mission statement is a vital part of any business, large or small. It should be specific and clearly articulate what you believe in and the quality of service that you will provide. Your mission statement should also speak to how people will feel after doing business with you.

While it is important to be specific when articulating your goals, it is also important not to get bogged down in methodology. A mission statement should be brief and to the point. It should be something that you can easily reference and that accurately captures the essence of your business.

Writing a mission statement may seem daunting, but it doesn't have to be. By following these simple tips, you can create a mission statement that will guide your business for years to come.

1. Start by articulating your core values. What does your business believe in? Why do you do what you do? Answering these questions will help you to identify the driving force behind your business.

2. Once you have identified your core values, you can start to craft a statement that reflects them. Keep it brief and to the point. Remember, you want your mission statement to be something that you can easily reference and that accurately captures the essence of your business.

3. Make sure that your mission statement is realistic. It should be achievable and reflect the current state of your business.

4. Finally, don't be afraid to revisit your mission statement from time to time. As your business grows and evolves, so too should your mission statement. By regularly reviewing and updating your statement, you can ensure that it always accurately reflects your business.

For my worksheet on how to craft your own mission statement, visit https://7daybusinessplan.com/workbook

1.3 DEFINE YOUR PRODUCTS AND SERVICES
Now that you know what your business is about, it's time to start thinking about what products and services you'll offer. This can be a difficult

process, but it's important to take the time to figure out what will work best for your business.

There are a few things to keep in mind when defining your products and services. First, you want to make sure that your products and services are relevant to your target market. You don't want to offer something that nobody wants or needs.

Second, you want to make sure that your products and services are unique. There's no point in offering the same thing as everybody else. You need to find a way to stand out from the crowd.

Third, you want to make sure that your products and services are affordable. Nobody is going to buy something if it's too expensive. You need to find a balance between offering a good value and making a profit.

Finally, you want to make sure that your products and services are easy to use. If your products and services are difficult to use, people will simply go elsewhere.

Keep these things in mind as you start to define your products and services. Take your time and don't rush into anything. This is an important decision for your business, so you want to make sure that you get it right.

Explain what you are selling. In detail. Not just what they are, but what they do. What does each service provide for your customer? What problem in their life does it solve? What does it make easier for them? What want does it fulfill? What are your product or service's unique features? What are the value added features to the end user? Are there any complimentary products/services that your product is dependent upon? What are they if any? How is your product/service positioned against the competition? What are you doing differently from what is on the market currently?

For my worksheet on how to outline the products and services that your business offers, visit https://7daybusinessplan.com/workbook

1.4 VISION

There are a few different ways that you can go about writing your company's goals and vision. One approach is to use 30-, 60-, and 90-day goals. This means that you set specific goals for each month and then track your progress. Another approach is to use a long-term planning method to outline your 1 year, 5-year, and 10-year goals.

We actually like to use both. This way, we can have both short-term and long-term goals to keep us accountable and on track.

No matter what method you use, it's important to be specific when writing your company's goals and vision. Vague goals will only lead to frustration and confusion down the road. So take some time to think about what you want to achieve and then put it down in writing.

If you need some help getting started, check out our goal setting worksheet, visit 7businessdayplan.com. It will walk you through the process of writing your company's goals and vision step-by-step. And if you're still feeling stuck, reach out to us and we'll be happy to chat with you.

Outline your 30-60-90-day goals. Primarily outline them as goals and objectives. Milestones that you can keep in front of you.

The first 30 days should focus on your learning and planning. While you can still be developing and selling product, your primary focus should be educating yourself about your market, learning your business, and developing strong plans. During this 30 days become a sponge, develop good business habits and practices that will become a part of your business culture.

The Second 30 days will be implementing the things that you've learned. Testing and analyzing the results and perfecting the implementation of your plans. This is where theory gets put to the test by actual practice. DOCUMENT EVERYTHING so that you can let the numbers make the decisions for you.

The Third 30 days are about a sprint to the next level. This is a demonstration of what has been learned, implemented and analyzed over the first 60 days. By the end of the 90th day, you'll have a baseline of things that are working for you. A consistent methodology that you can perform, explain, and teach when necessary.

The 30-60-90-day plan's goal is to put you in a place where your plans are set and your operations are defined. Of course, we know that business is ever changing, so these things aren't etched in stone. However, doing this will give you a level of comfort moving forward that "winging it" won't. You'll be amazed at the progress and accomplishments you make.

1-year goals – your first year is your most important year. You want goals that are attainable yet are challenging enough to make you WORK. This will set the tone for your business for years to come. Some examples of 1-year goals are:

1. Acquire funding
2. $400,000 in revenue
3. 5 profitable campaigns
4. Major profitable launch event

5-year goals – Five-year goals help to give you vision and keep you disciplined in moving forward through the tumultuous world of business. There are always trends, sales people, and market fulgurations that try to cause you to make decisions. You have to make sure that every situation you make is aligned with the goals you have set.

5-year goals should be as specific as possible and at least 3x your 1-year goals. You can also add new goals.

When writing out goals, whether they are short or long term, it is important to make sure they are SMART goals. This stands for Specific, Measurable, Achievable, Realistic, and Timely. Let's break down each one of these elements:

- **Specific**: The goal should be clear and specific, so that you know exactly what you need to do in order to achieve it.
- **Measurable**: The goal should be something that can be measured, so that you can track your progress and see how close you are to achieving it.
- **Achievable**: The goal should be something that is achievable, so that you don't set yourself up for disappointment.

18

- **Realistic**: The goal should be something that is realistic, so that you can actually achieve it.
- **Timely**: The goal should be something that has a deadline, so that you can stay on track and not let it drag on forever.

Chances are, this isn't new to you. However, it's important to be reminded. Keep these elements in mind when writing out your goals, and you'll be well on your way to achieving them!

If you need some help getting started, check out our goal setting worksheet. It will walk you through the process of writing your company's goals and vision step-by-step. And if you're still feeling stuck, reach out to us and we'll be happy to chat with you.

1.5   CONSEQUENCES & REPERCUSSIONS

Business goals aren't just a stand-alone product. We also have to understand that with every success or failure comes a reward, consequence, and repercussion. This helps to motivate us to accomplish the goals that we have set out. It also provides a sense of ownership for our actions and choices.

Business rewards & Consequences are different than personal ones. While personal rewards and consequences are often direct in nature (e.g., vacations, bonuses, fines etc.), business rewards & consequences are more external facing.

For instance, when we hit our business goals, it's important to celebrate success. We should also know what those successes are. For instance, hitting your target revenue goal for the year will position you as an industry leader. That's a business reward.

Conversely, our business consequences can feel more devastating. Let's say you don't hit that revenue goal, a business consequence can be lower valuation, having to lay off employees or worse.

While we will always stay optimistic, it is important that we stay cognizant of what "could be" so that we stay focused.

- **Positive Consequences**

It's good to identify the great things that will happen when you accomplish your goals. This gives you something to look forward to. Some call it your "why." This could include your family, mental health, peace of mind, even some luxuries that you hope to have earned. The key is, to have something to look forward to besides more work.

- **Negative Consequences**

I've learned that sometimes "negative reinforcement"

works. Now the negative consequences that are outlined aren't the cost of not fully reaching your goals. These are the cost of inaction, delayed action, and inadequate action. There's no need to go "gloom and doom" because we don't want you to be scared stiff and be more afraid than you need to be.

CONGRATULATIONS!!! You've made it through DAY 1!!!

Even if it took you more than a day, you've gotten through the first step in writing your business plan.

By now you have:

- Business name
- Mission Statement
- Product Description
- Vision and Goals

That's pretty dope!

Ok, take a quick break, and come back tomorrow ready to throw down!!!

Remember, if you haven't already, download your FREE companion workbook at https://7daybusinessplan.com/workbook

DAY 2 – DEFINE YOUR MARKET

THIS is probably the most critical part of your plan. The one that will drive you and every business move that you make. You will likely refer to your target market at EVERY TIME you think of developing a new product, acquiring a new business, or expanding your reach.

Knowing WHO you want to reach, what they like, what they dislike, how much they are willing to spend, how many children they have, what type of coffee they drink can all be critical to your business's decision making.

HOWEVER, done right, this piece right here will take a lot of the guess work out of planning and operating your business. As a business owner, it's important to have a clear understanding of who your target market is. Without this knowledge, it becomes difficult to create marketing and sales strategies that will effectively reach your desired audience.

There are a number of ways to define your target market. Perhaps the most common approach is to consider demographics such as age, gender, location, and income level. However, you can also look at other factors such as interests, lifestyle choices, and purchasing behavior.

Once you have a good understanding of who your target market is, you can start to create marketing and sales strategies that are tailored to their needs. This will help you to more effectively reach your desired audience and boost your bottom line.

If you're not sure how to define your target market, there are a number of resources that can help. For example, the Small Business Administration has a helpful guide on their website. You can also find plenty of information online from marketing experts.

When it comes to defining your target market, the most important thing is to have a clear understanding of who you want to reach. Once you know this, you can start to create strategies that will effectively reach your desired audience. By doing so, you'll be well on your way to boost your bottom line.

2.1   CREATE YOUR AVATAR

This is so important that it's the ONLY thing you'll be doing today – ENJOY IT.

When it comes to marketing, one of the most important tools you have at your disposal is your customer avatar. This is a semi-fictional representation of your ideal customer, based on real data and research.

Too often business want to target EVERYONE b/c if EVERYONE buys your product, then you'll make money, RIGHT? Well, targeting EVERYONE will likely leave you with very few customers outside of those who know and love you. At which point you'll be stuck in the "Friend Zone" making enough money to support your hobby; but not a business.

Defining your avatar means narrowing your target down to ONE PERSON that you are talking to. ONE PERSON that you want to please at every turn. You know EVERYTHING about this ONE PERSON. You know them better than you know yourself, and your ONLY goal is the please him or her.

Creating a detailed customer avatar will help you better understand who you should be targeting with your marketing efforts. In turn, this will help you create more effective and targeted marketing campaigns, resulting in better results.

So, how do you go about creating a customer avatar? Here are the steps you need to take:

1. Gather data on your target market. This can come from a variety of sources, including market research reports, surveys, and customer interviews.
2. Analyze the data to identify common characteristics among your target market.
3. Use these characteristics to create a semi-fictional representation of your ideal customer.
4. Use your customer avatar as a guide for all your marketing efforts, from crafting messages to designing campaigns.

24

By following these steps, you'll be well on your way to creating a customer avatar that will help you take your marketing to the next level.

There one key thing that you MUST remember when developing your Avatar:

YOU ARE NOT...I REPEAT NOT YOUR AVATAR

While you may share characteristics with your target market, don't just market based on what YOU LIKE. Go with the numbers, look at data, let the facts guide you. There are some things that you'll be able to "go with your gut" on, but this isn't one of them.

Here are things to consider as you develop your avatar:

Demographics – you must consider not only who NEEDS your product but also who is likely to BUY your product. We all have the tendency to make the mistake of thinking that our products are for everyone who needs them. However, the fact is, our products are for everyone who will PURCHASE AND USE them.

- Age
- Location
- Gender
- Income level
- Education level
- Marital or family status
- Occupation
- Ethnic background

Psychographics
- Personality
- Attitudes
- Values

- Interests/hobbies
- Lifestyles
- Behavior

You are not limited to the above criteria. These elements are just a broad starting point for you to define your target audience. Have fun with it. Imagine how your avatar acts when in the grocery store, their online persona, how they spend their free time. Personally, this is one of my favorite parts of business because it gives me the opportunity to step outside of myself and what I like and REALLY focus on SERVING.

Once I've gotten to the point where I KNOW what makes my target audience "tick" and even what "ticks them off", I am able to see opportunity at EVERY TURN. I walk in to my neighborhood Walmart, and not only am I thinking about myself and my family, I'm also thinking about my avatar, and if there is something that I have that can make their Walmart trip easier and/or more enjoyable, within the scope of my business model, of course. This isn't to say that my goal is to solve EVERY PROBLEM I see, but it does help to be able to focus and see outside of what is natural to me, and focus on my customers.

Once you have gathered all of this information, put it all together to describe, in detail, your target customer.

To download my customer avatar template, which includes resources to research your customer avatar visit https://7daybusinessplan.com/workbook

Side note – Market Segmentation:

At some point, it may be necessary to do market segmentation, where you break out your market based on more than one avatar so that you may serve them with more than one product. Don't worry about that now, but when it comes, it's a good thing because that means you're GROWING!!!

DAY 3 - INDUSTRY ANALYSIS

In order to be a good businessman/woman, it is important to know your industry. You have to know what business you are getting into. You must understand what it's like to operate a business in your industry; the key success factors, industry trends and of course, your COMPETITION. Most importantly, you have to be able to answer the question:

Why will my business succeed when others have failed?

This is where industry analysis comes in. Industry analysis is used to examine current and historical data in order to identify industry trends, opportunities and threats. It allows you to understand your place in the market and develop strategies to stay ahead of the competition.

Industry description and outlook

This is where you'll discuss the current state of your industry overall and where it's headed. Here, you will identify relevant industry metrics like size, trends, life cycle, and projected growth. This not only give your insight into what you're getting yourself into. It will also let banks or investors see that you know what you're doing, and have done your

27

homework and come prepared with the data to back up your business idea.

Talk about your industry as a whole (i.e., if you're a photography business focusing on weddings, focus on the photography business). You need to understand what it's like to operate in your industry.

- Describe what it takes to succeed in your industry (key success factors) in as specific terms as possible
- List and explain changes and trends in the industry (e.g., new technology or law) that will affect companies operating in your industry. Using the photography example, you'd want to highlight the growth of DSLR cameras and cellphonographers
- Who are the gatekeepers in your industry (if any)? (People or businesses that can give a business access to customers or suppliers in the industry

There are a few analysis methodologies that you can use to gather this data
Understanding these concepts will give you a solid foundation on which to build your business. Let's take a closer look at each one.

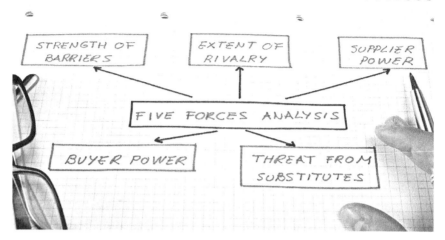

Porter's Five Forces Analysis

Porter's Five Forces is a model that identifies and analyzes the competitive forces that shape every industry. It is a tool used to understand how those forces affect an industry and its profitability.

The five forces are:
- Suppliers
- Customers
- Competitors
- New entrants
- Substitutes

Let's go into detail

Suppliers

The supplier's bargaining power is the extent to which they can control the prices of their inputs. If they have significant control, then they have high bargaining power. This can be due to a number of factors such as having a monopoly on the input or being able to produce it at a lower cost than competitors.

Customers

The customer's bargaining power is the extent to which they can control the prices of the products they buy. If they have significant control, then they have high bargaining power. This can be due to a number of factors such as having a monopoly on the demand for the product or being able to switch to a substitute easily.

Competitors

The extent of competition in an industry depends on the number and size of competitors, as well as the barriers to entry. If there are few competitors and/or high barriers to entry, then the industry is considered to be oligopolistic. This means that the competition is not as intense and companies have more control over prices.

New entrants

The threat of new entrants is the extent to which new firms can enter the market and compete with existing ones. If it is easy for new firms to enter the market, then the threat of new entrants is high. This can be due to a number of factors such as low barriers to entry or high customer switching costs.

Substitutes

The threat of substitutes is the extent to which other products can provide the same function as the product in question. If there are many substitutes, then the threat of substitutes is high. This can be due to a number of factors such as close substitute products or high customer switching costs.

SWOT Analysis

Most if not all business owners, even prospective business owners, are familiar with a SWOT analysis. A SWOT analysis is a tool that is used to identify the Strengths, Weaknesses, Opportunities and Threats of a business. It is a way to understand the internal and external factors that can impact the success of the business.

Instead of going into super deep detail about a SWOT analysis, I'm just going to provide some sample questions that you may want to ask yourself to get started.

1. Strengths (internal, positive factors)

The strengths of a business are the things that give it an advantage over its competitors. They are the factors that make the business unique and allow it to offer a better product or service.

Strengths describe the positive attributes, tangible and intangible, internal to your organization. **They are essentially within your control.**

- What do you do better than most?
- What internal resources do you have? These may include:
  - *Positive attributes of people*, such as knowledge, background, education, credentials, network, reputation, or skills.
  - *Tangible assets of the company*, such as capital, credit, existing customers or distribution channels, patents, or technology.
- What advantages do you have over your competition?
  - Do you already have a loyal base?
  - Patents & Copyrights
- Do you have strong research and development capabilities? Manufacturing facilities?
- What other positive aspects, , add value or offer you a competitive advantage?

2. Weaknesses (internal, negative factors)

The weaknesses of a business are the things that make it vulnerable to its competitors. They are the factors that make the business less effective or efficient. Weaknesses are aspects of your business that detract from the value you offer or place you at a competitive disadvantage. **You need to enhance these areas in order to compete with your best competitor and it's fully dependent on your business's efforts.**

- What factors that are within your control detract from your ability to obtain or maintain a competitive edge?
- What areas need improvement to accomplish your objectives or compete with your strongest competitor?
- What factors (expertise, access to skills, access to technology) does your business lack?
- Does your business have limited resources?
- Is your business in a poor location?

3. Opportunities (external, positive factors)

The opportunities for a business are the things that make it possible for the business to grow and prosper. They are the factors that create new market opportunities or allow the business to take advantage of existing ones. Opportunities are external attractive factors that represent **reasons your business is likely to prosper.**

- What opportunities exist in your market or the environment that you can benefit from?
- Is the perception of your business positive?
- Has there been recent market growth or have there been other changes in the market the create an opportunity?
- Is the opportunity ongoing, or is there just a window for it? In other words, how critical is your timing?
- Is there legislation (Local, State, Federal) being implemented that is in your business's favor?
- Is there a trend that you see emerging that others don't that you can benefit from?

4. Threats (external, negative factors)

The threats to a business are the things that could cause the business to fail. They are the factors that could make the business less competitive or even obsolete. Threats include external factors beyond your control that could place your strategy, or the business itself, at risk. **You have no control over these,** but you may benefit by having contingency plans to address them if they should occur.

- Who are your existing or potential competitors?
- What factors beyond your control could place your business at risk?
- Are there challenges created by an unfavorable trend or development that may lead to deteriorating revenues or profits?
- What situations might threaten your marketing efforts?
- Has there been a significant change in supplier prices or the availability of raw materials?
- What about shifts in consumer behavior, the economy, or government regulations that could reduce your sales?
- Has a new product or technology been introduced that makes your products, equipment, or services obsolete?

Competitive Analysis

This is where you discuss your competition in general and then focus in more detail on your main competitors. You can also discuss substitutes if they are relevant (e.g. trains vs. buses vs. short-haul flights compete for the same customers)

A competitive analysis is a tool that is used to understand the strengths and weaknesses of your competitors. It is a way to identify their key areas of focus and their areas of weakness. This information can then be used to develop a competitive advantage.

The first step in conducting a competitive analysis is to identify your competitors. This can be done by researching their websites, their marketing materials, and their product offerings. Once you have a good understanding of their business, you can then start to analyze their strengths and weaknesses.

One way to do this is to create a list of their key areas of focus. This could include their target market, their marketing strategy, their product offerings, and their pricing strategy. Once you have this information, you can then start to evaluate their strengths and weaknesses in each of these areas.

- Describe how competition is in your industry. Is it consolidated (where a few players control much of the pie like a few social networks like Facebook, LinkedIn, Pinterest, Twitter control) or it is fragmented (where there are many players and the largest ones still have a very small percentage of the total pie like furniture makers).
- Who are your main competitors? These are other options your customer would go to for a similar product/service at a similar price point.
- Describe the key metrics companies use to measure themselves on and compete with each other on (e.g. clothing companies

compete on design, distribution outlets, quality, and price) Note: these metrics should be closely related to the Key Success Factors you highlighted in the industry research

- Compare how you stack up next to your top competitors (ideally 2 to 5 competitors) using the key metrics

Another way to conduct a competitive analysis is to create a SWOT analysis for each competitor. This will help you to identify their strengths, weaknesses, opportunities, and threats. Once you have this information, you can then start to develop a competitive advantage.

Industry Analysis

An industry analysis is a tool that is used to understand the structure of an industry. It is a way to identify the key players in the industry and the forces that are driving the industry. This information can then be used to develop a competitive advantage.

The first step in conducting an industry analysis is to identify the key players in the industry. This can be done by researching their websites, their marketing materials, and their product offerings. Once you have a good understanding of their business, you can then start to analyze the structure of the industry.

One way to do this is to identify the forces that are driving the industry. This could include things like new technologies, changes in consumer demand, or shifts in the competitive landscape. Once you have this information, you can then start to develop a competitive advantage.

Another way to conduct an industry analysis is to create a PESTEL analysis for the industry. This will help you to identify the Political, Economic, Social, Technological, Environmental, and Legal forces that are impacting the industry. Once you have this information, you can then start to develop a competitive advantage.

- Political factors include things like government regulation and trade restrictions. Economic factors include things like inflation, recession, and interest rates.

- Social factors include things like changing demographics and social attitudes.
- Technological factors include things like advancements in technology and the impact of digital disruption.
- Environmental factors include things like climate change and pollution.
- Legal factors include things like regulation and intellectual property protection.

When assessing these factors, it's important to consider how they are impacting the industry both currently and in the future. For example, a recent recession may be causing problems for a particular industry right now, but if the economy rebounds, then that industry may see a resurgence. It's also important to consider how each factor could impact your business. For example, a new technology that disrupts your industry could have a major impact on your business model or even put you out of business.

Market Analysis

A market analysis is a tool that is used to understand the structure of a market. It is a way to identify the key players in the market and the forces that are driving the market. This information can then be used to develop a competitive advantage.

The first step in conducting a market analysis is to identify the key players in the market. This can be done by researching their websites, their marketing materials, and their product offerings. Once you have a good understanding of their business, you can then start to analyze the structure of the market.

One way to do this is to identify the forces that are driving the market. This could include things like new technologies, changes in consumer demand, or shifts in the competitive landscape. Once you have this information, you can then start to develop a competitive advantage

For my worksheet on Industry analysis visit 7businessdayplan.com/worksheet.

DAY 4 – MARKETING & SALES PLAN

No matter how good your product is, you'll only be successful if you can get it in front of people who not only can benefit from it but will pay for that benefit. There are a plethora social networks, search engines, and tools that exist on the market. And while each of them have their benefits, you'll never be able to maximize your advertising dollar without a plan. So before you even make your first Facebook ad, or Pinterest post, you'll have your strategy and test plan in place!

Here's what you need for a marketing and sales plan:

1. **Know your audience:** You can't be everything to everyone, so it's important that you know who your target market is. What are their demographics? What do they like? What do they need? Once you know these things, you can begin to create content that will appeal to them.

2. **Set your goals:** What do you want to achieve with your marketing and sales plan? Do you want to increase brand awareness? Drive more traffic to your website? Make more sales? Once you know what your goals are, you can start to develop a plan to achieve them.

3. **Choose your marketing channels:** There are a lot of different marketing channels out there, so it's important that you choose the ones that will work best for your business. Do some research and see where your target market is spending their time. Once you know that, you can start to develop a presence on those channels.

4. **Create or refresh your brand identity:** Your brand is what sets you apart from your competition. It's important that your brand is strong and consistent across all of your marketing materials. If you don't have a strong brand identity, now is the time to create one.

5. **Develop targeted content:** Once you know who your target market is and what they like, you can start to develop content that will appeal to them. This could be blog posts, social media posts, or even videos. Whatever form it takes, make sure that your content is interesting and informative.

6. **Invest in paid advertising:** Paid advertising can be a great way to reach your target market. But it's important that you do your research first. You don't want to waste your money on ads that no one will see.

7. **Analyze and adjust course as needed:** Once you've implemented your marketing and sales plan, it's important to monitor the results. See what's working and what isn't. Adjust your plan accordingly and continue to track your progress. By following these steps, you can create a marketing and sales plan that will help you achieve your goals.

Today you will:

- Develop a summary of your marketing message
- Identify and describe current offline marketing methods
- Identify and define current online and social media marketing vehicles
- Identify and define additional offline marketing strategies
- Categorize all of your current and future marketing materials
- Describe your optimum sales force
- Develop your marketing and sales plan.

You're FINALLY able to use a shortcut (if you have it available. You can refer to:

- Your current marketing Materials, (Flyers, brochures, emails, etc. that have been used.)
- Current Marketing Budget and/or expenses

- Your sales team description
- Sales history
- Sales forecasts
- Testimonials

4.1 MARKETING MESSAGE

Your marketing message is NOT about you and your product. It's about your customer's needs and desires. You product or service is simply the vehicle that help the fulfill their needs and desires. If you're a photographer, you don't want to talk about you and your camera equipment. You want your message to talk about the BENEFITS of having a professional photographer with your camera and equipment.

Much of what you will be writing in your marketing message will be based on the work you performed developing your avatar. In each of your marketing materials, you will want to use different combinations of your pain points, pleasure triggers, and make sure that you are positioning your solution as the answer to both.

For instance, Apple doesn't tout their processor power, they talk about the speed and ease of use that if provides its users. For years they didn't even talk about the features of the phone (except in those meetings that Steve Jobs led) they simply said "There's an app for that." That was the entire push. In just those five words, Apple said they would eliminate pain, and/or give you pleasure at the same time. If you want pleasure, there's an app for that. If you want to avoid pain, there's an app for that.

Of course, they have millions of dollars that they spend on focus groups, studies, etc. that you may not have at this time.

However, that doesn't mean that you can't implement the same concept to market your business.

First, in 45 words or less, describe how you position your company in the market? How do you want potential customers to think of your business? Take a few minutes are write it down. Here's an example.

Prototype Promotions provides Best-in-class photography services that capture moments that last a lifetime. From our Weddings, portraits, and events; to our "Person Paparazzi" services, we not only provide you quality photos, we provide you a quality experience. Put down the cell phone, WE GOT YOU!

I purposefully wrote that message in less than 4 minutes. Just to test myself. Now it may take you more or less time depending on how well you know your business and your customers. In writing that, my desire was to SHOW that we can fulfill ANY photography need (Listing known services), CREATE intrigue (what is Personal Paparazzi?) and mystery, and RELATE to the customer's current situation (Stop taking pics w/ your cell phone)

Some call this an "Elevator pitch". Either way, it's necessary to be able to succinctly define and be able to communicate your marketing message.

4.2 ONLINE MARKETING

Now that you have summarized your message, now we want to explain your plan for getting your message and name out to the masses. Online Marketing is an ever-evolving phenomenon that can broaden your customer base and rake in huge profits. Online marketing includes websites, search engines, banner ads, and of course social media.

Next you will outline each of the online marketing avenues you plan on using. Remember, ESPECIALLY when it comes to social media, you will need to come up with separate plans based upon how each network is used by consumers. (e.g., Customers use Facebook in a completely different way than they use Snap Chat)

Below is a list of possible Online marketing opportunities (at the time of this writing):

- Social Networks (Facebook, LinkedIn, Instagram, Twitter, etc.)
- SEO
- PPC/PPI ads
- Review Sites (Yelp)
- Company Websites
- Email campaigns
- Blogs
- E-Commerce sites (industry determined)

List each of the avenues that you will use to advertise. Don't forget to also include how much and how often you plan on using each method.

ALERT: IF YOU HAVE NOT DOWNLOADED OUR COMPANION GUIDE DO IT NOW!!!! That is where this list and more current strategies will be updated.

4.3 OFFLINE MARKETING

While online marketing is, any many cases, less expensive and has a farther reach than online marketing, it's pertinent that you do not ignore offline marketing techniques. They have been working since the dawn of time.

Here, you want to describe where and how often you will advertise. Below, outline your methods of offline advertisement to include (but not limited to) Posters, Brochures, Print Ads, Billboards, Customer Loyalty programs, coupons, Broadcast Media, etc. how much it will cost, and how often you plan on using them (you will need these numbers for your financials).

Here are a few offline marketing ideas to get you started:

1. Direct mail

Direct mail is still an effective way to reach your target market. By sending targeted postcards or brochures directly to potential customers, you can increase brand awareness and generate leads.

2. Print advertising

Print ads in newspapers and magazines are another great way to reach your target market. Placing ads in publications that your target market reads will help increase brand awareness and drive traffic to your website or store.

3. Public relations

Generating positive press coverage is a great way to increase brand awareness and drive traffic to your website or store. By working with journalists and pitching story ideas, you can get your business featured in magazines, newspapers, and online publications.

4. Trade shows and events

Attending trade shows and events related to your industry is a great way to generate leads and build relationships with potential customers. exhibiting at trade shows can also help increase brand awareness for your business.

5. Networking

Meeting new people and networking with potential customers is a great way to generate leads and build relationships. Attending industry events, joining professional organizations, and participating in local Chamber of Commerce meetings are all great networking opportunities

4.4   ADDITIONAL MARKETING & SALES STRATEGY

While your primary focus will be on the online and offline marketing; you may also want to explore additional strategies, which include:

- **Strategic Partnerships:** working with other companies with similar target markets to cross-promote in order to expose your product to additional potential customers and even make sales. Strategic partnerships are a great way to get your product in front of new potential customers. By teaming up with other companies that have similar target markets, you can cross-promote and expose your product to a whole new audience. And, if you have a good affiliate program in place, you can even make sales through these partnerships.

- **Affiliate programs:** Affiliate marketing can be an extremely effective way to grow a business. By working with other companies that have similar target markets, businesses can expose their products to a larger audience and make sales more easily. In addition, by establishing affiliate programs, businesses can pay customers to help promote their products and services. This can create a mutually beneficial relationship between the business and its affiliates, which can lead to increased sales and improved relationships.

- **Licensing Agreements:** Licensing agreements are another great way to get your product out there. By licensing your product to other companies, you can tap into new markets and reach new customers. These agreements can be very beneficial for both parties involved.

4.5   SALES TEAM

Now while you may be a team of one right now; it's good to at least outline how you will run your sales team when you get one.

There are basically 3 types of sale representatives. You want to identify how u will use each.

- **Inside Sales** – Individuals who make sales based while on company premises. This includes sales floor, telemarketers and inbound call marketers.
- **Outside Sales** – teams who visit potential customers and nurture ongoing relationships; Often referred to Customer Relations.

Independent Sales Reps – These are independent contractors who sell your product across a large territory.

When it comes to each of these types of salesmen, you want to answer the following questions:

1. What are the highlights of their experience?
   a. Years
   b. Track Record
2. How do you pay them?
3. How do you train and motivate them?
4. What is their 'job' status within your organization? Full-time Employees? Independent Contractors? Affiliates?

In this day and age, there are a number of "For-hire" sales teams that will perform almost every portion of your sales process (Lead generation, initial contact, follow up, close) for commission or a flat fee plus commission. There are some that will perform the process for just a flat rate, however they wouldn't have 'skin in the game' which could be a risk.

4.6   PRICING

I know most business plans will start the financial section with the four major reports in a company's finances. And I'm going to do that later in this chapter. Many don't even discuss your pricing and pricing strategy. BUT we're not her JUST to build your business plan, it's to build your organization.

What REALLY matters to you is how to make sure you're making a profit. While it may take time for your balance sheet (we'll get there) to reach what is called "The black", you want to know how much it costs to run your business and how much you should charge for your products. These are the numbers you'll ALWAYS want to have a grip on.

The first thing you'll want to do calculate the cost of operating your business.

Direct Costs: Costs that are directly related to your goods and services that you provide. (Labor, Marketing, Manufacturing, etc.)

Indirect Costs: Also known as the "Cost of Doing Business" includes expenses used to keep the business running day to day. These include salaries, rent utilities, debt service costs, return on investment capital, office supplies, and other operating expenses.

This will give you a baseline of what is needed to keep the doors open

You have to know what the range of what you can sell

One key to determining how much you need to charge, is knowing how much you can handle. As you are first starting, chances are it's a one or to man (or woman) shop, in which you wear most of, if not all of the hats. Of course, you are on the road to changing that (remember, we're not just building a business, we're building an organization.) But for now, we are going to recognize that you ARE HUMAN and you have to crawl before you walk. That being the case, find out how much you can produce in a given period. For me, I look at it per week for an example.

Let's assume that I have just one product. Today, I'm going to use my "Fix Your Tie" sessions; bi-weekly sessions I have with entrepreneurs where we identify easy fixes that will make your job easier, your business stronger, and your profit larger. Each session is 1hr. I also spend about <2hrs researching your business and industry so that I'm prepared to provide valuable input. I also don't do these session back to back b/c time may run over. Finally, I do believe in work life balance, so I only have 10hrs set aside for client delivery.

So for each FYT booking here's what we have:

- Session – 1hr
- Prep – 90 minutes
- Buffer – 30 minutes

In this case each booking accounts for 3hrs. which means that I can do 3 FYT sessions per day. Since I work 6 days per week. I can do a max of 18 FYT sessions per week.

With this quick and easy formula, I have determined that I have the current capacity to do 18 sessions per week. So I would either have to make sure that my 'sweet spot number' (price) is enough to cover my costs, OR I would need my own FYT session, so that I could make some tweaks to the process.

All in all, the main reason for this portion, is to identify capacity for production.

Know your 'sweet spot number'

In the beginning, one of the many things you'll want to be certain of is that you price your goods and/or services so that when you are at minimum operations, these will be covered. This means that your **minimum price x minimum output = cost of operating business** (as discussed above).

Some people break it into the business and hit that sweet spot and just know the 'magic' number that they need to charge. Just know that is a HUGE anomaly, so properly identifying this baseline will not be an easy task. It may be that initially your 'sweet spot' number will be reliant on your maximum output. This part can be frustrating because on paper, you'll begin to question if this is really going to work and if it's will you lose. I've been there. Don't let it get you down because as I stated, we can work a few kinks out, look at some cursory improvements or even make some upgrades that will quickly turn everything around.

Also remember, we DID include YOUR SALARY in our operating costs so you won't starve. And when it comes to profit, there are some SIMPLE and LEGAL tricks that the "big boys" use that most of us don't even pay attention that will make sure you not only make profit but you also SEE profits.

Calculate your price

When calculating your price, you don't just want to go by how much it costs you. You also NEED to consider what it's worth to your customer. Think about it. Do you think that [insert your favorite brand here] prices solely based on the cost of doing business? Not ever close. They pay based on how much they believe that someone will pay for it.

Here are a number of pricing models that you can use:

- **Cost+ (Cost plus) pricing**

    This is probably the most common way of pricing. It's easy, simple, and relatively effective; likely the most straight forward approach

    Here, you add up ALL the costs related to the research, development, creation and delivery of your products and/or services, including materials, management, labor and overhead, then add a markup to arrive at a final price.

Pro tip: This approach is ideal for businesses needing a pricing strategy that's simple to implement, or if you have a cost advantage (i.e., achieve lower costs vs. competitors) and want to use price as a differentiator.

- **Value-based pricing**

Value-based pricing applies a price depending on your customers' perceived value of your offerings.

The higher the value perceived in your product or service, the more you can charge.

Value-based is one of my favorites and many in my field because of how we strive to bring value to our customers and clients. While some of my services may not cost me a lot, value-based pricing allows me to account for the savings, revenue, time, and efficiency that I bring to their organization; which is often exponentially larger than what they pay.

One good thing about value-based pricing is that as you continuously provide value to clients and customers, the actual and perceived value increases; giving you the opportunity to increase your price.

- **Skimming pricing**

Price skimming is great for businesses with built 'fans' who anticipate the arrival of their products. This is when, at launch, a product's demand is so great, that it is sold at its highest price; then lowering the price once the next model is released.

This is often done with cell phones, (especially iPhones) and video games where being early adapters comes with advantage or prestige. There was a time when this was also done with sneakers. There would be lines around the corner to purchase the newest Jordans and the price would be at its peak. (Since then shoe companies have moved to a scarcity model)

This works best when you have a customer base that is not price sensitive. They care more about having the product than how much it will cost them.

- **Premium pricing**

Premium pricing takes skimming pricing to the next level. It's luxury based. Premium pricing does not drop significantly when a new model is released. Rather the business will simply raise the price of the new offering.

For instance, you'll never see an inexpensive Rolex watch or Louis Vuitton bag; just a 'less' expensive one. With both, and many luxury brands, part of the brand is the high-quality and high price; it makes them more attractive (and in many cases duplicated)

- **Economy pricing**

Economy pricing is focused delivering the lowest price to consumers. Economy pricing is often dependent on having a broader reach and selling high volume. The most notable of economy priced models is Walmart. They are known for their low prices. Their brand relies on the fact that almost anyone can be their customer, so they can sale high volume and make a profit.

You'll also notice economy pricing with store/generic brand foods that don't rely on heavy advertising and frills, rather on being NEAR brands that do advertise and presenting a cheaper alternative.

- **Freemium pricing**

A combination of *free* and *premium*, the freemium pricing model is where the initial product or service is given to customers for free. With the caveat that there will be an upsell at some point in the future that will give access to full or extended features.

The freemium may lack a number of advanced features, expire after specified amount of time, or in some cases require extra assistance or consultations to fully take advantage of (useful but incomplete). In order to take full benefit of the freemium, the customer must pay.

Look at America Online's 600 hours disc (or CD-ROM) that would inundate your mailboxes in the 90s and 2000s as a great example. Or if that's a little to primitive for you, think about Dropbox's free version that upsells to a 1-2 terabyte storage plan for a fee.

- **Promotional pricing**

  This strategy involves offering a product or service, usually over a period of time, at a hugely discounted price a coupon or another type of limited time offer. The goal is to generate a sales boost by attracting customers to an irresistible offering for at a drastically lower price than what's normally available.

  This is the strategy that I use with most of my new business clients using my "Profit Accelerator". As it gives them the ability to engage their customer base using "Groupon" strategies without acquiring Groupon fees. For more information visit www.4daystolaunch.com/7days

- **Subscription pricing**

  This is where the customer agrees to pay a recurring fee (usually monthly or annually) to get access to a product or service. This is a popular pricing strategy today because businesses can obtain a predictable, recurring revenue source.

Many streaming services employ a subscription strategy.

- **Wholesale pricing**

  Wholesale pricing is a strategy used to sell your offerings to resellers or wholesale distributors at a rate lower than selling directly to consumers so that these other businesses can do the selling for you. This often includes bulk pricing as well. You wouldn't want to implement wholesale pricing for one-off sales.

- **Other pricing strategies**

  There are a myriad of other pricing strategies out there. Probably a whole book's worth (hmmm). I've just listed some of the most popular and used by entrepreneurs just starting out.

  Here are some other pricing strategies that you can consider:

  - Marginal-Cost
  - Absorption
  - High-low
  - Target Pricing
  - Price Leadership
  - Dynamic Pricing
  - Psychological Pricing
  - Penetration Pricing
  - Limit Pricing

  Here are some questions you should ask to help determine your price (in addition to knowing your costs). I know this my trip you out a bit; but bear with me (you're going to need your avatar for this one).

  Qualitative:

  - What is the intrinsic worth to your client/customer? (On a scale of 1-10 how positive is the effect on their life?)

  - How long does this affect last

- How easy is it for the affect be recognized?

- What is the cost to the client if they DON'T get what you need (On a scale of 1-10, how deep would the impact be if they did not receive what you have?)

- How long is that impact?

Make sure these questions are taken into consideration when you are doing your pricing exercise this will help to determine the percentage that you will mark up and establish your profit margins.

From a formula standpoint; what you'll want to initially identify the following. (and you'll be using these numbers in your other statements)

- Costs of goods/services sold
- Equipment
- Education
- Location
- Taxes
- Insurances
- Marketing

Monitor your prices and adjust accordingly.

With all this preparation, research and analysis, you should have all of the information you need to calculate the prices for your products and start selling. As we mentioned above, you might choose to incorporate multiple pricing strategies or adopt certain strategies for your individual product, business, and industry.

Remember, the most important thing about this is that you've successfully learned HOW to price a product. Your pricing process is not over. As time grows, you'll almost certainly change your prices. You may even choose other pricing models.

Be prepared to make adjustments as market changes occur. This ranges from competition, supply chain changes, and operating costs.

This being said, as you perform research, evaluate your costs, and consider possible profits, you'll want to carefully weigh all the factors we've laid out here. When it comes down to it, however, it's likely that you'll want to err on the side of higher prices (but also keep pricing transparency in mind). Many entrepreneurs tend to charge too little for their products, especially when they're just starting out.

Plus, it's always easier to lower prices than to raise them, and the market will provide a quick correction if you overshoot the mark with your strategy. Therefore, whether you're brand-new to business or a seasoned veteran, your effort and your ingenuity are probably worth more than you realize—don't be afraid to trust your instincts and set your prices accordingly.

For my worksheet on Marketing & Sales Plan
visit,7businessdayplan.com/worksheet

t.

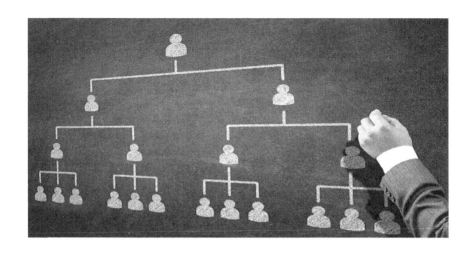

DAY 5 – MANAGEMENT STRUCTURE & OPERATIONS

As with anything you build, you'll want to have an infrastructure. Depending on the maturity of your business at this point, this may be fully fleshed out or just a blueprint. If you are at the point where this is just a blueprint, your may want to massage this before presenting it to potential partners and investors.

5.1   MANAGEMENT STRUCTURE

Your goal for this section is to demonstrate that you have the key personnel in place to increase your chances at initial and long-term success. If you are in the infancy stages and/or still operating as a one- or two-man (or woman) shop; a solid understanding of the leadership and key personnel needed to be successful will suffice for this section.

Start with no more five or six key personnel (including you as the founder) that you feel are critical to your team. These should be VP, C-level and Deputies. It's best to use conventional, recognizable titles as possible. Here are some positions to consider (this list isn't exhaustive and may vary based on industry):

- Founder

- President/CEO
- CFO
- COO
- CTO/CIO
- HR
- VP of Sales

For each of these positions you'll want to outline the experience, qualifications, and job descriptions clearly. Here are some questions your key personnel/management section should answer

- What role in the business does this person play (include intangibles).
- What education (Degrees, Certifications, etc.) qualifies them for this position?
- Any past performance and successes that have prepared them for this position
- What strengths can you highlight?
- Do they have equity or any other financial investments in the business?

In the case where there is an individual that you consider key personnel, but they don't have the experience or documented success that an investor would look favorably on, it's best not to do a lot of embellishment. You may want to consider not including them in this section.

5.2 OPERATIONAL STRUCTURE

This section outlines current and perceived positions within your organization. Again, this will show that you have a grasp on what is needed to be successful long term. While currently you may be wearing multiple operational 'hats' it's important that you have a plan to remove those hats in order to take a more visionary and leadership position.

While the chart above is great to show the structure, you may want to consider also including a narrative and/or flowchart that walks the reader through how these positions work with each other.

5.3 OPERATIONS

Now it's time to show that you KNOW your stuff. This means your product, service, etc.; essentially HOW you're going to run your business. Here you will describe how you perform the basic functions of your business. It's important to identify EVERY portion of your operations; even those that are outsourced.

You'll want to focus on your competitive advantages and how you achieve them along with highlighting any parts of your process that increase your profit margins, make your processes more efficient, and cut costs (as this is what partners and investors look for).

Operations include:

- Production
- Quality Assurance
- Location
- Facilities
- Distribution
- Fulfillment
- Customer Service
- Equipment
- Financial Controls
- Social Responsibility
- Technology

DAY 6 – FINANCES

Yes, you knew we were going to get here somehow, someway. You were either looking forward to it or dreading it. There's no in-between. Can you guess which category I fall into?

Well, no matter what category you fall in to; whether this was the part you were anticipating or thinking about skipping, this is a VERY important chapter. And one I hope to make easy for you.

Finances are what you're doing this for, right? If you're not in this to make money, then you're not in business, you're in hobby or charity. Both are fine, but MAN (or woman), have you gone a long way for nothing...Just kidding...I think.

Now down to brass tax.

Financials are the first thing that potential investors or lenders will look at when you approach them. If you've ever watched the tv show "Shark Tank" you've noticed that without a doubt, Mark Cuban (my mentor in my mind) or one of the other "sharks" will ask the question "What do the numbers look like?" This is because, no matter how excited an entrepreneur is about a product or service, or even how good of an idea it is, if the financials aren't reflecting this alleged greatness, then there is something wrong. HOWEVER, if the numbers are 'good'. Investors will be knocking down your door. Not to mention the amount of peace-of-mind that you will have.

The good thing is that it's not as complicated as you may think. And while as your organization matures, this will likely be something that you aren't hands-on with, it is important that you, at the onset, really understand the financial infrastructure of your business as you are ultimately the one responsible for your business. THE BUCK STOPS WITH YOU

6.1 PROFIT & LOSS STATEMENT (AKA INCOME STATEMENT)

This statement essentially shows whether your business is profitable. This is the most the most relied upon of all of your financial statements. The P&L, as it is sometimes called, is a summary of revenue and expenditures that shows whether or not your business is profitable. This shows total sales minus ALL expenses until you reach what is commonly called your "Bottom Line."

Your P&L statement includes the following

- **Gross Sales** – Total sales from all products
- **Allowances** – Deductions and/or discounts afforded to customers and deducted from the invoice (speedy payment, accepting faulty merchandise, high-volume purchase, etc.)
- **Commissions** – a percentage of the money received from a total paid to the agent responsible for the business He gets a commission for each car he sells.
- **Returns** – A return is the change in price of an asset, investment, or project over time, which may be represented in terms of price change or percentage change. A positive return represents a profit while a negative return marks a loss.
- **Net Sales** – Total sales after deducting paid commissions, returns, and allowances

- **Cost of Goods (COG)** – Costs of materials, inventory, etc. directly associated with production
- **Depreciation** – amount allowable for tax purposes for wear and tear of fixed assets
- **Net income** – income after deducting the cost of doing business
- **Net Profit** – Net Income minus taxes
- I know this may not make complete sense right now. Which is why I've given you templates. I know for me it became a lot easier once I started doing it, as opposed to reading about it.

6.2   CASH FLOW PROJECTION

Cash Flow Projection differs from a P&L statement and balance sheet (which we will touch on soon) in that it focuses on how much you have going in and out of the bank on a daily basis. This shows how long you can keep your doors open and pay your bills. If you business has a large inventory, sells on credit, or is primarily seasonal, this is extremely important.

Even if you're profitable, if you carry large inventory, or there is a lag time between delivery and payment, your bank balance may still reflect a "Cash Crunch." This can especially happen with businesses that are just starting as you may have to purchase materials for production long before you receive payment for finished product. There are ways to help alleviate a cash crunch. Yet in order to do that, you have to KNOW that it's coming.

Here are items to include in your Cash Flow Projection

- **Cash Sales-** Income received immediately for goods and services (cash, check, credit card) that will be deposited immediately or guaranteed within a short number of days.
- **Collections** – Accounts receivables from a previous period
- **Interest Income** – Cash received from interest bearing accounts
- **Loan Proceeds** – Cash received as a result of taking out a loan or using a line of credit

- **Equity Capital Investment** – Cash received from equity investors
- **Owner's draw** – Money paid to owner outside of salary
- **Ending Cash Balance** – Money in bank at beginning of recording period (Same as Opening Cash balance of next period)
- **Opening Cash Balance** – Money in bank at the beginning of the recording period

6.3 BALANCE SHEET

The balance sheet often a "snapshot of a company's financial condition". It shows what your business is worth at a moment in time; especially if it had to be sold. It demonstrates, for management, lenders, investors etc. the value of all property and the extent of all debt held by the business.

Here are the items to include in your balance sheet:

- **Fixed Assets** – Tangible property that your business owns that can be converted into cash. This could be equipment, cars (and other vehicles) computers, software, furniture and fixtures
- **Current Assets** – Property that can be quickly converted to cash. This includes inventory, accounts receivable, debtors, pre-paid expenses, investments, and of course actual cash-in-hand

It's not always easy to tell the difference between fixed and current assets. Here is a table that can help you to quickly identify what class your assets fall into.

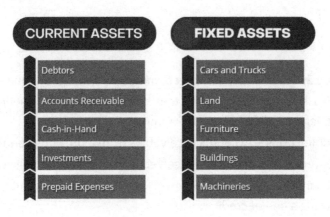

- **Current Liabilities-** obligations, accounts payable, bills, debts, etc. that must be paid of soon
- **Long term Liabilities** – financial obligations that must be paid over time; including auto loans, mortgages, equipment loans and other loans
- **Net Worth** – Easy! Assets – Liabilities = Net Worth
- **Paid in Capital** – Capital received from investors.

Let's be real, you didn't really want to read this chapter to look at the boring spreadsheets. Chances are you're going to hire a CPA to do these anyway. What you REALLY want to know is "How am I going to FUND my vision?" We're about to dive into the FUN stuff - so keep reading!

So now that you know a little bit more about financial statements and their importance, it's time to move on to the really exciting stuff – how to fund your vision! We'll be discussing different types of funding sources available and exploring how to best leverage them to ensure success. So get ready, because its time to dive into the world of financing!

So let's talk about funding sources. There are many different types of funding available to small businesses, such as loans, grants, and investments. Each type of funding can provide the resources needed to help you reach your goals. We'll discuss each type in depth so that you can decide which one is best suited for your business.

➤ **Banks and Lending Institutions**

Loans are a common source of funding for small businesses and can come from lenders such as banks or credit unions. The loan amount and terms will vary depending on the lender, but they typically require collateral (such as a house or car) in order to secure the loan. Loans often come with interest rates that must be paid back over time.

What they look for:
- Good credit score
- Collateral
- Ability to Repay
- Clear plan for repayment

One of the advantages of banks and lending institutions is that they don't ask for equity, shares in profit, or even a say in how you run your business. All that a bank is interested in is getting their money back with interest.

Some drawbacks to getting a loan from banks and lending institutions is that the interest rates can be high or the application process can take quite some time to go through. Additionally, they often require collateral in order to secure the loan.

➤ **Family and Friend loan**

Another type of funding available to small business owners is a loan from family or friends. This type of loan often comes with little or no interest and flexible repayment terms, making it an attractive option for those who don't want to deal with the hassle of dealing with banks and lenders.

The downside to taking out a loan from family or friends is that it can put a strain on personal relationships if payments are not made in a timely manner, so it's important to be mindful when considering this type of financing. Additionally, there may be legal implications if the loan is not documented properly. So before you move forward, make sure you have a written agreement specifying the terms of the loan.

➢ Government Grants

Government grants are another popular source of funding for small businesses. These grants are typically awarded to businesses that are engaged in activities that meet certain criteria and can be used for things like research, marketing, or capital investment. The amount of money available and the criteria for eligibility vary from program to program.

The advantages of applying for government grants are that they don't need to be repaid and can provide a great source of additional funding for your business. The downside is that it can take quite some time to get approved and you must meet certain guidelines in order to be eligible for the grant. Additionally, there may be restrictions on how the money can be used.

➢ Investment and Crowdfunding

Another type of funding available to small businesses is investment or crowdfunding. Investment is when a person or group invests money into your business in exchange for equity, while crowdfunding is when you raise money from the public via an online platform. Both of these types of financing require that you offer something in return – either shares of your company or pre-sale rewards – so it's important to think carefully about what kind of offering would best suit your needs.

The advantages of investment and crowdfunding are that they can provide much needed capital to get your business off the ground as well as exposure for your brand through marketing campaigns and promotions. Additionally, if successful, these campaigns can result in a large influx of cash. The downside is that they require a lot of work and may not be successful if there isn't enough interest in your offering.

➢ **Business Credit Cards**

Finally, business credit cards can also be a great source of financing for small businesses. Business credit cards provide convenience, rewards and benefits, as well as flexibility when it comes to repayment terms. Furthermore, they are often easier to obtain than traditional loans since lenders don't require any collateral or proof of income and the application process is usually quick and easy.

The disadvantages of using a business credit card is that they come with high interest rates and fees if payments are not made on time. Additionally, there may be limits on how much you can spend each month so it's important to understand your spending limits in order to avoid incurring too much debt.

➢ **Investors**

Another option for financing your business is to attract investors. Investors are typically individuals or organizations who provide capital in exchange for equity in your business. They may also provide additional resources such as advice, contacts, and sometimes even mentorship.

What they look for:

- Strong leadership team
- A clear plan for generating returns on their investment
- Risks/rewards of their investment clearly defined

One major benefit of obtaining funding through investors is that you don't have is that banks and lending institutions can be quite stringent with their criteria for giving out loans. The requirements are often difficult to meet and the process of getting a loan can take months. In conclusion, you REALLY want to ensure that when it comes to finances, that you have determined what types of financing you are willing to take on and how it works in your favor.

In searching for financing answer the following questions:

QUESTIONS TO PONDER	YOUR ANSWER
How much, if any equity & ownership are you willing to give up?	
How much control are you willing to give up?	
What, if any, properties are you willing to risk to start your business?	
What type of interest rate & terms are you willing to accept?	
How much can you realistically borrow?	
How large do you want your company to be?	
How fast do you want to grow?	
Are you willing to have long-term relationships with funders or investors?	

DAY 7 – A DAY OF REST!!!

After all your hard work, you deserve a day of rest. This is the perfect time to reflect on all that you've accomplished and set your sights on future goals. Take this day to relax, recharge, and renew your commitment to your business. If God Himself rested on the seventh day, surely you can too!

Why even call this a 7 day plan if on the 7th day you aren't doing anything? Easy, because most of time, if we don't plan to rest, we WON'T! We entrepreneurs are a different breed. We typically pour our heart and soul into whatever it is we're doing, so much so that rest usually gets pushed to the back burner or skipped altogether. That's why scheduling a day of rest as part of your business plan can be so beneficial.

Taking time for yourself helps you to stay focused and productive when executing your business plan. It also allows you to reset and refocus on the task at hand. When rested, you can think more clearly, plan better, and work smarter.

So when it comes to your business plan, don't forget to include a day of rest! Schedule it in, take the time off and enjoy what the day has to offer. You'll be glad you did! Rest is an essential part of your success, so don't neglect this important step in your business plan!

It takes time to build a successful business. It's not just about setting up the framework and executing on one day; it's a process that requires dedication and passion over an extended period of time. Day 7 is all about taking a step back and reflecting on what you've accomplished so that you can make informed decisions for the future.

After a long week of work, planning, research and preparation, it's important to take some time for yourself. Dedicate this day to relaxation and reflection. You've accomplished a lot, and it's important to celebrate your successes. At the same time, look ahead to future goals and what you want to achieve. This is a day to renew your commitment to your business and charge yourself up for the coming week.

You may be tempted to work on this day, but resist the urge. It's important to have a day of rest, just as God did after creating the world. Use this time to recharge your batteries and come back refreshed and ready to begin to implement this great plan you've created!

How to "Rest" on the 7th Day

Although this day is all about resting, that doesn't mean you have to do nothing. Here are some ideas of how to make the most of your seventh day

- Spend time with family and friends: This is a great opportunity to catch up with loved ones and enjoy some quality time together.
- Get outside: Take a walk, go for a hike, or just spend time in nature. Fresh air and vitamin D can work wonders for your mental and physical health.
- Do something creative: Use this day to tap into your creative side. Paint, write, scrapbook, or whatever else inspires you.
- Catch up on sleep: Get a goodnight's sleep and wake up feeling refreshed and ready to start the week ahead.
- Oh...yes...it's ok to do NOTHING

No matter how you choose to spend your seventh day, make sure you take some time for yourself. This is a day to relax, reflect, and renew your commitment to your business. You've worked hard all week, and now it's time to recharge your batteries. With a little rest and relaxation, you'll be ready to tackle anything that comes your way!

You'll be ready to take on whatever comes your way tomorrow. Thanks for following along with our 7-day business plan! We hope it's helped you get started on the right foot.

We hope you've enjoyed this 7-day business plan. If you have any questions or comments, please feel free to reach out to us. You are even entitled to a FREE consultation ($500 Value). Simply visit https://discovery.launchwithcarl.com

FIN

Made in the USA
Middletown, DE
22 June 2023

33112034R00046